STEGOSAURUS

A Buddy Book
by
Michael P. Goecke

ABDO
Publishing Company

VISIT US AT
www.abdopub.com

Published by ABDO Publishing Company, 4940 Viking Drive, Edina, Minnesota 55435. Copyright © 2002 by Abdo Consulting Group, Inc. International copyrights reserved in all countries. No part of this book may be reproduced in any form without written permission from the publisher.

Printed in the United States.

Edited by: Christy DeVillier
Contributing editor: Matt Ray
Graphic Design: Denise Esner, Maria Hosley
Cover Art: Patrick O'Brien, title page
Interior Photos/Illustrations: pages 4, 6, 8, 9 & 11: Patrick O'Brien; page 17: Denise Esner; page 18: ©Douglas Henderson from *Riddle of the Dinosaurs* by John Noble Wilford, published by Knopf; page 21: Rich Penny, www.dinosaur-man.com; page 23: Deborah Coldiron; page 25: M. Shiraishi ©1998 All Rights Reserved.

Library of Congress Cataloging-in-Publication Data

Goecke, Michael P., 1968-
   Stegosaurus/Michael P. Goecke.
      p. cm. – (Dinosaurs set II)
   Includes index.
   Summary: Describes the physical characteristics and behavior of the plant-eating dinosaur Stegosaurus.
   ISBN 1-57765-635-0
  1. Stegosaurus—Juvenile literature. [1. Stegosaurus. 2. Dinosaurs.] I. Title.

QE862.O65 G64 2002
567.915'3—dc21

2001027932

TABLE OF CONTENTS

What Were They?..4

How Did They Move?...8

Why Was It Special? 10

Where Did It Live?...12

Who Else Lived There? 16

What Did They Eat? 20

Who Were Their Enemies? 22

The Family Tree 24

Discovery 26

Where Are They Today?....................................28

Fun Dinosaur Web Sites 30

Important Words 31

Index 32

WHAT WERE THEY?

Stegosaurus
STEG-uh-SOR-us

The Stegosaurus was a plant-eating dinosaur. It lived about 150 million years ago. That was during the late Jurassic period.

The Stegosaurus was about 26-30 feet (8-9 m) long. That is almost as long as a school bus.

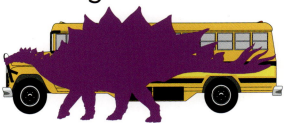

The Stegosaurus weighed about 6,800 pounds (3,084 kg). That is heavier than a rhinoceros.

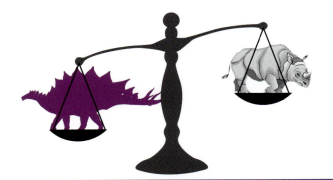

The Stegosaurus's name means roof lizard.

The Stegosaurus had a tail with four spikes. Each spike was about four feet (one m) long.

This dinosaur's head was small for its body. Its brain was small, too. The Stegosaurus's brain was about the size of a Ping-Pong ball.

How did they move?

The Stegosaurus walked on four, thick legs. Its back legs were longer than its front legs. So, its head was close to the ground.

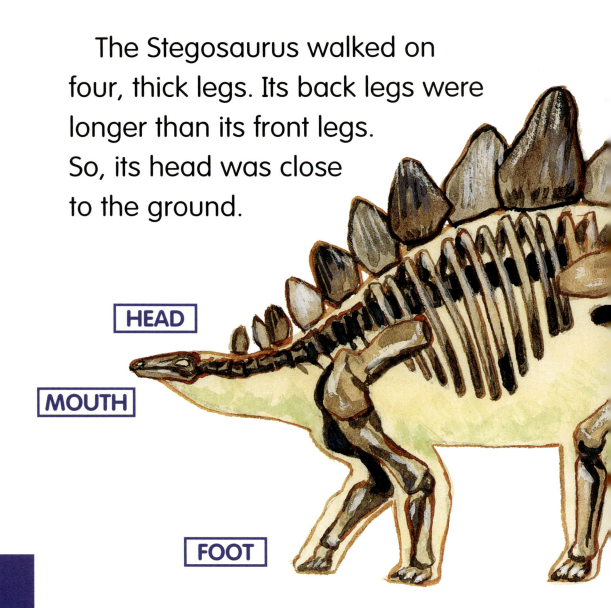

HEAD

MOUTH

FOOT

This huge dinosaur walked slowly most of the time. The Stegosaurus could not run very well. It fell down if it ran too fast.

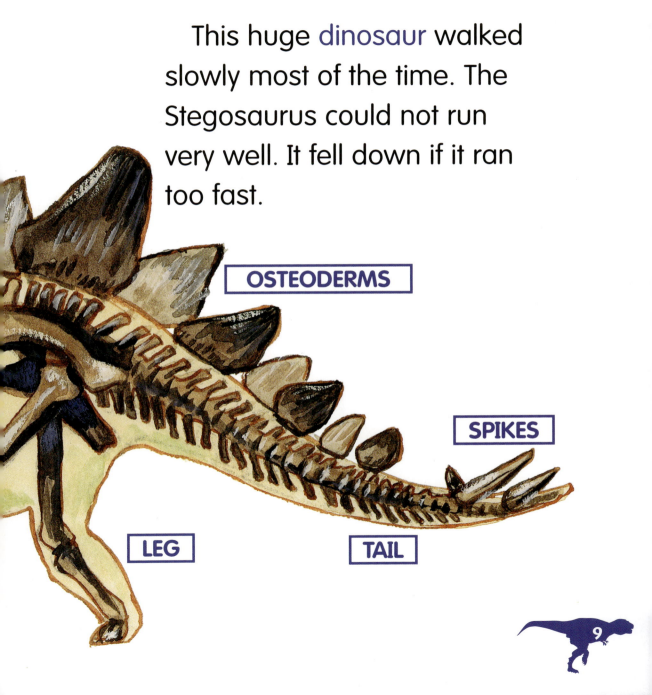

WHY WAS IT SPECIAL?

The Stegosaurus had bone plates on its back. We call these plates osteoderms. These osteoderms stood on end. They looked a little like triangles. The Stegosaurus's osteoderms made its back look like a saw.

Can you find the Stegosaurus's osteoderms?

The Stegosaurus probably used these osteoderms to warm and cool itself. The osteoderms caught sunlight. This warmed the Stegosaurus. In the shade, cool air blew across the osteoderms. This cooled the Stegosaurus.

WHERE DID IT LIVE?

The Stegosaurus lived all over the world. It lived in North America, Europe, India, Asia, and Africa. People have found Stegosaurus fossils in Colorado, Utah, and Wyoming.

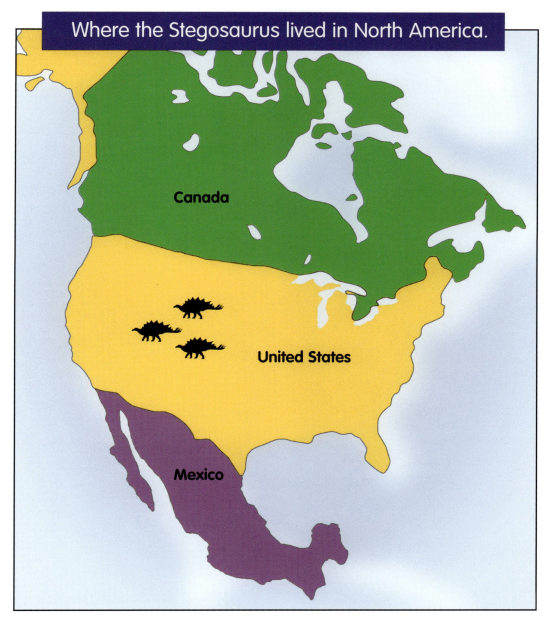
Where the Stegosaurus lived in North America.

The Stegosaurus lived in forests.

The world was a warm place when the Stegosaurus lived. There was no ice at the North Pole or South Pole. Also, there was a lot of water on the land. This water made many lakes, rivers, and oceans. The water and warm weather helped large forests to grow. These forests gave food and cover to the Stegosaurus.

WHO ELSE LIVED THERE?

The Stegosaurus lived among other dinosaurs. One was the Othnielia. The Othnielia ate plants. It was only about four feet (one m) tall. The Othnielia walked on its two back legs. Its front arms were small.

The Othnielia

The Diplodocus ate plants.

The Diplodocus was another dinosaur neighbor of the Stegosaurus. It was a very large plant-eater. It weighed as much as 40,000 pounds (18,144 kg). That is heavier than three elephants.

WHAT DID THEY EAT?

The Stegosaurus did not have a long neck. It could not reach high into trees. So, this dinosaur ate plants off the ground. The Stegosaurus ate plants like ferns and mosses. It may have eaten small, bushy trees, too.

The Stegosaurus ate with a beak. There were no teeth in this beak. Instead, there were teeth on the sides of the Stegosaurus's mouth.

The Stegosaurus ate plants off the ground.

WHO WERE THEIR ENEMIES?

The Stegosaurus had to be careful of carnivores, or meat-eaters. Carnivores hunted the Stegosaurus. The Torvosaurus was a carnivore. It weighed about 4,000 pounds (1,814 kg). That is not as big as the Stegosaurus.

The Torvosaurus was a carnivore.

The Torvosaurus was a good hunter. It was quick and powerful. This carnivore used its claws and huge teeth to catch the Stegosaurus. The Stegosaurus may have used its spiked tail to fight back.

THE FAMILY TREE

There were different kinds of stegosaur dinosaurs. The stegosaur dinosaurs had osteoderms and spiked tails. The Stegosaurus was the biggest stegosaur.

Stegosaurus

Paranthodon

Kentrosaurus

The Kentrosaurus and the Paranthodon were stegosaurs. They lived in Africa. The Kentrosaurus had spikes on its tail like the Stegosaurus. The Paranthodon had osteoderms and spikes on its neck, back, and tail.

The Kentrosaurus

DISCOVERY

The Dacentrurus

The first stegosaur fossils came from England. These fossils belonged to the Dacentrurus. Frederic A. Lucas named the Dacentrurus after its spiked tail.

In 1876, M.P. Felch found the first Stegosaurus fossils. He found them in Colorado. Othniel Marsh named the Stegosaurus in 1877.

Where Are They Today?

Smithsonian National Museum of Natural History
10th Street and Constitution Avenue
Washington, D.C. 20560
www.nmnh.si.edu/paleo/dino

Honolulu Community College
874 Dillingham Boulevard
Honolulu, HI 96817
www.hcc.hawaii.edu

American Museum of Natural History
Central Park West at 79th Street
New York, NY 10024
www.amnh.org

Carnegie Museum of Natural History
4400 Forbes Avenue
Pittsburgh, PA 15213
www.cllpgh.org/cmnh

STEGOSAURUS

NAME MEANS	Roof Lizard
DIET	Plants
WEIGHT	6,800 pounds (3,084 kg)
SIZE	26-30 feet (8-9 m)
TIME	Late Jurassic Period
ANOTHER STEGOSAUR	Kentrosaurus
SPECIAL FEATURE	Osteoderms, spiked tail
FOSSILS FOUND	USA—Colorado, Utah, Wyoming Europe, India, China, and Africa

The Stegosaurus lived 150 million years ago.

First humans appeared 1.6 million years ago.

Triassic Period	Jurassic Period	Cretaceous Period	Tertiary Period
245 Million years ago	208 Million years ago	144 Million years ago	65 Million years ago

Mesozoic Era · Cenozoic Era

29

FUN DINOSAUR WEB SITES

ZoomDinosaurs.com
http://www.enchanted learning.com/subjects/dinosaurs/dinotemplates/ Stegosaurus.shtml
A detailed look at facts and ideas about the Stegosaurus.

BBC Online – Walking with Dinosaurs – Fact Files
http://www.bbc.co.uk/dinosaurs/fact_files/bigal/stegosaurus.shtml
Information from the Discovery Channel series "Walking with Dinosaurs." Details about the Stegosaurus.

Dinosaurs
http://www.cfsd.k12.az.us/~tchrpg/Claudia/Steg.html
Basic information about the Stegosaurus including behavior, habitat, and activities for children.

IMPORTANT WORDS

carnivore a meat-eater.

dinosaur reptiles that lived on land 248-65 million years ago.

fossils remains of very old animals and plants.

Jurassic period period of time that happened 208-146 million years ago.

North Pole the northernmost point of the earth.

osteoderms bone plates that grow on stegosaur dinosaurs.

South Pole the southernmost point of the earth.

spikes the long, sharp objects at the end of the Stegosaurus's tail.

INDEX

Africa, **12, 13, 25, 29**
Asia, **12**
beak, **20**
Canada, **13**
carnivore, **22, 23**
China, **29**
Colorado, **12, 27, 29**
Dacentrurus, **27**
Diplodocus, **18, 19**
England, **27**
Europe, **12, 13, 29**
Felch, M.P., **27**
fern, **20**
fossil, **12, 13, 27, 29**
India, **12, 29**
Jurassic period, **4, 13, 29**

Kentrosaurus, **24, 25, 29**
Lucas, Frederic A., **27**
Marsh, Othniel, **27**
Mexico, **13**
moss, **20**
North America, **12**
North Pole, **15**
osteoderm, **9-11, 24, 25, 29**
Othnielia, **16, 17**
Paranthodon, **25**
South Pole, **15**
spike, **7, 9, 23-25, 27, 29**
Torvosaurus, **22, 23**
United States, **13**
Utah, **12, 29**
Wyoming, **12, 29**